A Cadence For Redemption

Conversations with Abraham Lincoln

Eve Wood

DEL SOL PRESS.
A CADENCE FOR REDEMPTION
Copyright © 2022 by Eve Wood
All rights reserved.

Printed in the United States of America.
Del Sol Press, 2020 Pennsylvania Avenue, NW,
Washington, D.C., 20006.
www.delsolpress.org
ISBN: 978-1-7344900-4-6

Cover Art by Robert Gunderman
Title Page Artwork by Brian Pellar
Interior Art by Robert Gunderman and Eve Wood

Our books may be purchased
for promotional, educational, or business use.
Please contact Del Sol Press by e-mail at editor@delsolpress.org.
First Edition: May 2022

10 9 8 7 6 5 4 3 2 1

i

I have an irrepressible desire to live till I can be assured that the world is a little better for my having lived in it.

- Abraham Lincoln to Joshua Speed

For My Father

Table of Contents

7:10, AM, April 14, 2020

Breakfast

He orders black coffee.
Drinks seven cups.
I hand him a napkin
And he wipes his wide mouth.

There is nothing I know
That he hasn't imagined,
His face like burled wood,
His eyes seated in their own inspiration,
The simple wisdom of the trees,
The fierce, incongruous wind.

He smiles to encourage me
As the eggs bleed-out on the plate
And the coffee turns to black earth.

I would like to say something, anything,
Though the moment does not allow for this,
So I sit in flawed admiration
As above us jet planes
Tunnel the sky, spewing
Chemtrails, the leavings of a dead
And unrecognizable world,
And the silence between us
Like a luminous gift.

Finally, he sets the small cup in its cradle
And his voice takes the air
As though the earth itself whispered:
"The greatest among you are the most fragile."

8:45 AM, April 14, 1865

My Face in the Woodpile

I was raised to chop wood,
To carry the heaviest bucket of water
For a distance undisclosed,
But to which I've since
Become accustomed.
Ambition is a slow amble,
Insinuating itself softly into the folds of my life
Until the pursuit of truth, defending the lives
Of thieves and murderers, discrediting
The moon with a simple almanac,
No longer held my attention.
I could just as easily have been one of those men,
But for the two silver trees
That came to me one night in a dream,
Proffering destiny with the falling
Of each argent leaf.
I was held captive inside my own mind,
And I knew it would always be so,
My only peace,
Forever whittling down
The long line of years
To find my own face in the woodpile.

9:34, AM, April 14, 2020

Late Morning Coffee

I long to escape the world,
Inhale the rarified air in deep space,
But I would settle for a conversation
With a kind-hearted man.

I long to fly high
In the district of seagulls
Or dive into the harrowing sea,
But I could just as easily
Eat a peach or pierce
A puddle with the head of a stick.

Once I tried to explain the miracle of fire
To a woman who'd made a stone
Of her heart,
But all I could hope for
Was the sun moving westward
Across the densely amplified sky.

10:12 AM, April 14, 1865

A Heel of Bread

Bread has a strange integrity,
A staying power
As nations rise
And sink back
Into oblivion.

There is always a heel of bread,
The leavings of a last and final feast,
A means of sustaining our indelicate lives.

I aspire to its simple prerogative
To keep us alive,
Carried in a knapsack across the blasted fields,
Or deep into the forest.

I could learn my life over
With each daily meal,
The controlled purpose of the blade
As it cuts through the soft, risen dough.

10:22 AM, April 14, 1865

Acquiring Distance

The oval office brims
With the advancement of new light,
Lemon-colored, softer
On the carpet nearest the door
Like an exquisite meringue,
Then the sudden shift
To darkness, the depth
And complexity of marmalade.

What is justice
And what does it mean to be alive?
And what of the theater of light?
It is only a tool to live by,
To weigh the persistence of morning
Against the presumption of an early slumber.

The light acquires distance,
Shifting in and out of crevices
As it expands over the floorboards
The way a man's life pushes out
Across the long years.

There are points of entry
And moments of departure,
Not all sacred,
But each divine.

2:00 PM, April 14, 1865

The Men Who Surround Me

The magic of good government belongs
To more than one man.
The industry of warfare – all that we give
In exchange for our freedoms
Is a machine like any other,
A group of disparate men
With hands in their pockets and notes
In their hats, chewing on Cuban cigars,
Transforming
Shared vision, together
Deciding the future
With
One
Solid
Aggregate
Purpose.

12:35 PM, April 14, 1865

The Better Angels of Our Nature

Who are we to determine the weight of any man's soul
As equal to a stone,
Or for those we deem "lesser men"
If men at all, something
Even less?

We are all helpless
And alone from the day we draw breath
To the moment we surrender that breath
To the air.

We are all lopsided
In the face of death,
Staggering backwards
To plant our feet one last time
In the earth.

So, who are we to sell another man's life
On the auction block
For the price of a pygmy goat,
To sanction the miraculous
And profit from despair?

Daily, our saints and demons
Whisper their stories of joy and defeat,
The better angels of our nature
Forever standing guard
At the gates of our sad
And ever-shattered lives.

12:48 PM, April 14, 1865

To Prevaricate is To Be Human

Sometimes I pause
Too long at the threshold of my thoughts,
The knowledge that I too will pass from the living world
Like a single musical note
Hung on the air for a moment
Before slipping into the cacophony of sounds.

One might say I am too much with myself,
But it is not simple mindfulness
That fixes me here,
Since to prevaricate is to be human,
But each day, imperfect and unique,
Strung until a garland
Of years
Is made

To be broken.

1:01 PM, April 14, 1865

On the Subject of Joshua Speed

Like bees to the honey pot,
The rumors abound,
Every aspect of my life framed
Under glass, magnified
In air-tight compartments
Beneath the stilted gaze
Of history, but I am not
Here to balance a silver dollar
On the tip of my nose,
Or salivate on command –
I loved that man
The way feathers encompass a bird,
Or the night yields the darkness
Into dawn.
You can insist it was the work of the body,
But sometimes the soul flies without us --
A feeling beyond comprehension
As always in a room full of headaches
There must be
Some means of letting go.

2:22 PM, April 14, 1865

The Bomb of Shame

I may be a knock-kneed wayfarer,
A monstrosity by the physical standards
Of the day, bowing my head
Each time I enter a room,
A gnawing shame at the base of my neck
That radiates out into the rest
Of my form, but I am
Pale as birch bark,
And this fact alone sets the tenor
And arc of my life --
The law -- my inheritance,
Not unearned,
But the road
Was joined with ivory.

Emancipation was only a word
Laced with black blood.

I proclaimed, not for the sake of violence or necessity,
But because one day I went
Walking and turned
A sharp corner into
The ever-darkening shade of my life,
My own derelict shadow,
Forever standing guard
Over nothing.

Lunch

There he is, sudden,
As a change of weather.
He carries a thin and crusty paper sack,
Opening it to reveal an avocado and a few tired grapes.
I feel his lucidity,
A temporary balm
To quell the fever
I live by.
The limbs of his body,
Their length and musculature,
Antecedent to the heavy oak
And the slender forearms of the birch.
What is it he wants from me
And why does he sit so near?
Perhaps the ghost of him echoes
The ghost in me, a hollow, indeterminate place,
A moment of indecision or regret,
Yet within every shadow, every ghost,
Beats the wings of a fearsome, primordial bird
Long gone under in the soul,
That finally,
And for the last time, extends
Its wings across
The clear, virgin sky.

2:45 PM, April 14, 1865

Stove Pipe Hat

Like everyone, I have moments
Of strange apprehension,
Periods of joy and unrest,
Unrealized dreams
And off-color jokes,

And you ask why my hat is so tall?

2:58 PM, April 14, 1865

Gettysburg

Over and over in the barbarous night
I sing the chaste song of my heart
And am strangled by each waking dream of war.
Only the morning is my friend,
Lighting my way
To the sturdy
Responsibilities of the day,
And for a short time, I am safe,
Until behind me, rising
In the long shadow
Of the Capital,
Six hundred thousand young bodies
Bleed out,
As I wade back
Through the darkness
Again.

3:34 PM, April 14, 1865

To Lydia Bixby
(upon losing five of her sons in the war)

I am afraid only the trees
Stood witness to the falling
Of each of your boys,
Taking the field as they did,
Young lions laying down
Their soft heads in the grass.
But I've heard word from the flowering dogwood
And the cypress as well
That the battle-worn birds
Flew so low and into the fray,
They stole each boy's final breath
And made it their own
To bear it away on the wind.
It's true. I wasn't there,
And who would trust the knowledge of trees?
But step outside
On any windswept day
And make their breath
Your own.

3:41 PM, April 14, 1865

Depression

Imagine wrapping your brain in muslin
And standing in a tunnel for thirty years,
Yet you must always hold a smile to your face
Just as the trees hold the leaves to their branches
Or the water encompasses the wide mouth of the dam,
And remember an ant's life is to itself as sweet
As ours is to us.
Perhaps my radical gloom
Was milk sick, the cows having eaten
Poisonous roots, and the poison
Never left me.
Whatever it may be,
The rain's insistence scares me
More than the jackal at my door,
And never do I carry
An open blade in my pocket.

3:46 PM, April 14, 2020

Afternoon Tea

I am trying to immerse myself in the scope of your life
Like a swan drunk on the fate of the river.
I feel your heart power
Through me, whispering
"Though I am satisfied,
I discern an anxiousness
That I cannot hope to diffuse,"
And again, I am struck
By the weighted splendor of my grief,
Which is much more than I expected,
Though far less than the barbarous losses
That strangely sustained you.
I am attempting to understand
The ritual of sadness,
Couched as it is between joy
And surrender.
Like you, gentle and relentless,
I am living
My best life
In the dashed
All-encompassing current.

4:14 PM, April 14, 1865

Fox in the Snow

Justice is like this –
It's there, but you have to squint
To see it.

Snow collects on her nose,
The frigid mantle of fur,
Indistinguishable from the landscape.
The simple traveler narrows his eyes
Toward nothing
But the vehement cold,
And the fox just a few feet in front of him.

Only when the man falls,
Hard and alone,
Enveloped in the bitter armor
Of winter,
Do his eyes adjust
To the animal at his feet.

4:31 PM, April 14, 1865

In Advisement of the Human Soul

What is courage?
Does a man wake
To it suddenly,
Aware one day that an eagle,
Unlikely and ill advised,
Extends its wings
The entire length of his soul?
What is goodness?
Does it take root over time
Like music softly lulling
The heart toward
Its better intentions?
What is kindness,
But all the windows in the house
Blown open.
Or patience, that friend who sits
At your bed-side long after
The tremors
Have passed.
Why are all the essential
Human qualities busted open
And bleeding out on the streets
Of our cities?
Was integrity only ever a fever dream,
The one I kept to myself
For too long?

4:42 PM, April 14, 1865

On What It Means to Be President

Imagine an invisible thread that extends
From the center of your chest
Out into the hearts
Of every man, woman and child,
Weaving a diaspora of intersecting lives.
Imagine the responsibility of trying
To give voice
To that formless human yearning,
Knowing each person's life is a song,
A specific cadence for redemption,
And it is your job to optimize
The circumstance by which they might
Be heard, if not with their own language,
Then by yours.
Imagine attempting to apprehend
The intricacies of human desire,
The whispered longings
Of thirty million, then
Channel those longings
Through your own feeble heart
In the hopes they might one day
Feel recognized.

5:50 PM, April 14, 1865

The Great Birds of Springfield

Great birds threaten me
From the hills of Antietam
To the stairs of this intrepid House,
Yet I cannot be
Everything to everyone, my life
Like the face of a clock without hands,
Propelling me forward, yet
Blind to each moment.
A soldier once asked me
Where birds go
When they die,
And all I could think to say
Was the perfect orchestrations of heaven
Are conducted on the wings of a dove.

5:58 PM, April 14, 2020

Twilight Scotch

I feel my own incongruence
As the Scotch pulls me into its orbit,
And I wait beneath the rubber tree
For Lincoln to convince me
Everyone has their limits.

Whether he or I was born
Out of time
Is of little consequence,
Each of us
Drunk
On the knowledge
Of the other.

6:02, PM, April 14, 1865

A Brief Reminiscence

Those to whom evil is done
Reciprocate evil in return; those
Whose teeth chatter in the deep night
Of their heads have a clue
What it is to die.
The world keeps breaking,
And my dreams of serenity
Drain out like rusty buckets
At a baleful parade.

Every one of us has a riot
Behind our eyes, an invisible
Demarcation between the violence
We level at ourselves
And the unfairness we bring to the world.

Into this libidinous air we continuously
Hope to thrive, to engender
Tenderness in the hearts
Of those who are newly arrived.
Into this tenuous balance
We attempt to tip the scales
Yet again.

Once more I stand here, seduced
By my shadow which tells me
To labor fervently in the service
Of darkness when I know
The truth of everything
That is beautiful.

The lights must burn on forever,
And the constant eruption of stars must be

The bright music of our future.
Only by this blessed and rigorous orchestra,
Are we made
And unmade again.

6:31 PM, April 14, 1865

To Mary Todd Lincoln, My Apologies

Tonight, there's no movement beneath your door
As I stand in wide-eyed ignominious delight
Of nothing and of no one,
But you.
Now I understand how the wolves
Chart their lives by the moon,
Setting the tenor of their hearts
To a burgeoning aperture of light.
You are waning,
And dark as I am, I come once again
To sit beside you,
Shuddering, immersed in the din of my blood,
So brutal and alone, a scarce, half made-up man
Seeking justice.
It's a wonder
You are here at all, harangued
By ghosts
And the unsullied lives
Of the children of who've gone on before you.

But this is a love poem, Mary, not
A chilly approximation of despair,
And because this may be as close
As I will ever come to voicing
The strange admonitions of my heart,
Listen as I whisper
At your perfectly closed door
That my darkness is the singular scoundrel of my life,
Absorbed as it is in the light
Which is yours.

7:26 PM, April 14, 2020

Dinner

Leaning back in the stiff wooden chair,
And extending his arms the length
Of a country table,
He tells me he doesn't eat meat
And can't abide sugar.
I imbibe.
He does not, opting
Instead for warm milk.
The questions I ask are obvious –
Until finally something important
Occurs to me –
And I ask--

"What does it mean to have compassion?"

Beneath his angular frame
The chair scrapes the floor
As though to answer in his stead –

"Compassion is listening,
Even as the blood trickles down from your ears."

8:43 PM, April 14, 1865

The Brigade

There is no fairness in the endless brigade of black bodies,
Wading through their own sweat
In the sweet withering fields.

Shallow-figured, they come to me
In the deadest hour of night,
The inherent shade of their skin
Indistinguishable from the resolute dark.
I listen to the perfect pitch of voices
Closing the chasm
Between the living and the dead,
But like a tree that's lost its middle,
The leaves rock high and away on the breeze
While below, the trunk breaks
Clean with the earth.

When I awake, the morning has turned gray
And I remain rebounded
To the solipsism of my mind,
Knowing the next night will bring the voices,
And I will beg
Their forgiveness again.

9:21 PM, April 14, 1865

Wee Willie Wallace

The night you ascended, wee Willie Wallace,
The sky cleared a pathway between the clouds
As the gaping jaws of heaven took you in.

The rain needled my face as I stood in the drive
Beneath the looming façade,
The stringent architecture
Of the great White House.

I apologize for the séances,
The spirit mongers,
The gypsies and the saints,
Sitting vigils for months,
Claiming to draw you down from the stars.

I apologize if your mother keeps
Your death mask at the side of the bed,
Referring to it constantly,
Nor can I blame you for rising
So wild and high,
But you must understand, dearest boy,
That you alone were the wind in the branches,
And every apple in the field.

10:00 PM, April 14, 2020

Late Night Snack

The day Lincoln died, his spent blood
Formed the image of a bridge on the pillow,
A seemingly endless outflow
Of proteins and plasma, each rivulet
Expounding
The seepage of history –
The ambitions of science—
The carnage of war –
And always and everywhere
People falling
In and out
Of love.

10:26 PM, April 14, 1865

Like everyone else, I heard the popping
Seconds before my own shuddering
Blood closed me down.
My dream of flying
Over the ocean faster
Than the speed of light
Unfurls
And suddenly
There I am,
Floating over the bannister
And into
The belly of The Ford.
Below me, the frozen moment
Cracks open -- the heavy
Barrage of scented flesh
As people scatter,
Women dropping painted fans
And men falling forward.
My coattails vanish
And the sinister weight of my head
Turns to air.
Like a struck doe, Molly wails,
Her grief no longer my concern.
Somewhere deep in the bowels of the theater
A small but luminous breach begins
To pulse with light.

You all know how I entered,
But where in God's name have I gone?

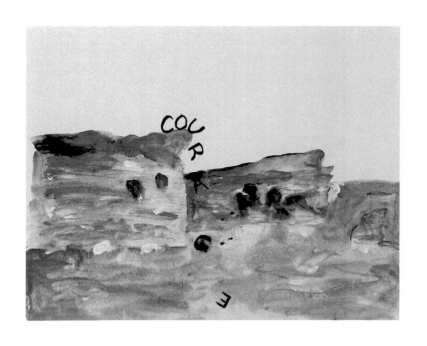

11:59 PM, April 14, 2020

Milk at Midnight

Oh, honest Abe, I dreamt
You were standing behind me,
Guiding my hand
The way a child holds a kite steady
In the windswept sky,
And for a moment the world was healed.

These days, tenderness is a word
I rarely pronounce,
For in my house
There is no other language,
Screaming beauty to the rafters
And my lover's high polished shoes.

Oh, honest Abe,
Was that half pound of tea
Really worth it,
The six miles there
And the ever-darkening journey back?

I feel your answer like the wind through the leaves:

"When the apples in the orchard,
Bruised and bleeding on the earth,
Dishonor themselves to the trees,
We must all gather them,
Not with wretchedness,
But with love."

2:49 AM, April 15, 1865

Molly Me

Some of us marry sorrow –
Not for a moment, an hour
Or even a day, but
Hotly it chases us down
The full length of our lives.

I am one,
And she is another,
Bookending the same dismal sky.

Three boy's dead
And now me into the mix,
This four-cornered specter
Hovers over her bed,
And when she awakens, our faces
Flicker momentarily before her eyes
Like a wide blanket pulled
Once again across the sky.

She claims crickets serenade her
Deep into the night
As she crosses over the silver bridge.

Some of us marry sorrow,
An importunate bride
Who trembles
All joy from our souls.

Oh, Molly me,
Cinch for good
Your torrent of tears
To see, finally, how much
I love you.

2:57 AM, April 15, 2020

A Final Glass of Water

I tried to keep the visits secret,
But hiding Lincoln
Was like muffling the voice of a giant with silk.

I needed answers,
And he, entombed in eternity,
Was appalled to wake up
And discover the bastardization
Of all he held dear.

Crouching into the room,
He bumped his head on the ceiling
And the world I once loved
Began to crumble.

The sun lay capsized in the fields,
And even the moon slipped
Her moorings in the dark, felted sky,
Sliding into the sea
Like the long-awaited whisper
Of a friend who died
Young.

6:45 AM, April 15, 1865

The Boarder Willy Clark

Lucky for me you were out that night,
Those dominoes burning a hole in your pocket;
Even in that you played to win.
You must have been exhausted
To fall so sound asleep
On the bloody bedsheets
Where my body lay,
But I can assure you I was aware
Of your predicament, even
In my twilight, slipping away
From logic toward the unknowable
Distance between myself
And the rising sun,
I was thinking of you Willie Clark,
Making your way across town
Like a spark seeking refuge in dry wood,
Looking for love or trouble.
Either way, the world
Is incontestably your own.
Perhaps you're a man untouched
By superstition, married
To the here and now,
The wine on your table,
The woman on your arm,
But history cannot be denied –
The fact a small piece of my body
Was left behind on your crimson pillow,
And you simply closed your eyes
And turned over.

7:22 AM, April 15, 1865

A Sudden Dispensation of Light

This bright firmament is the storm upon which I ride
My life out, soaring
Over the headlands into
The breaking dawn.
The blue opalescence of clouds blinds me
For an instant, and the top of my head,
An arrow, aching for the sky, that pierces
The lingering fog.

In the distance, a flag set high on a hill
Snaps hard on the wind,
And it is then I see laid out before me
A field of rising blood,
618,000 eyes laid open to the sky,
Fixed in cold astonishment.

A sudden dispensation of light,
A beam, so high and pure,
Carries me higher still,
But I must take my place beside them
In the fractured asylum of the earth,
The deepening soil,
Alive with fat and honorable worms.

3:33 PM, November 7, 1865

Stealing Lincoln

Eleven years and five minutes from today,
They will try to lift
My narrow bones from the crypt
Where for too long those walls kept me
Safe.

Only a man who forges counterfeit nickels
Could presume such extravagance,
And isn't a bullet to the back of the skull enough
To satisfy the slavish interests of men?

Really, what is left for us if a man can plot
The theft of another man's body,
And not understand
He has desecrated,
Not only the sacred bones of the dead,
But his own feeble soul?

4:54 PM, April 14, 1922

Upon Construction of the Lincoln Monument

Someone left a half-eaten bagel on my toe.
The crows pick it apart with their beaks,
And I am more amazed with their industry
Than with any human achievement.

I know better than most
The vindictiveness alive
In the hearts of men
As still my ghost wanders the parapet
Overlooking the gardens
Of the noble White House.

See here -- my nose,
Absurdly long, and might well serve as a fencepost,
And really, I had no idea
My eyebrows were wide as hedges.

None of this seems necessary,
And the fact of it
Makes me queasy.

The hands of the men who mined this marble
From steaming Georgian quarries,
Might, under different circumstances,
Have written a verse perhaps
Or pulled a dying man
From a fire.

I can think of a thousand better pastimes
Than smoothing the jagged contours
Of this face.

THE END